SKIMMERS

SKIMMERS

by Downs Matthews • photographs by Dan Guravich

SIMON AND SCHUSTER BOOKS FOR YOUNG READERS

Published by Simon & Schuster Inc.

New York • London • Toronto • Sydney • Tokyo • Singapore

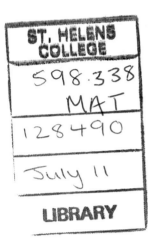

SIMON AND SCHUSTER BOOKS FOR YOUNG READERS
Simon & Schuster Building, Rockefeller Center, 1230 Avenue of the Americas, New York, New York 10020.
Text copyright © 1990 by Downs Matthews. Photographs copyright © 1990 by Dan Guravich. All rights reserved
including the right of reproduction in whole or in part in any form. SIMON AND SCHUSTER BOOKS FOR YOUNG READERS
is a trademark of Simon & Schuster Inc.

Designed by Lucille Chomowicz Manufactured in the United States of America 10 9 8 7 6 5 4 3 2 1

Library of Congress Cataloging-in-Publication Data: Matthews, Downs. Skimmers / Downs Matthews;
photographs by Dan Guravich. Summary: Describes the life cycle of the black skimmer and how one particular flock
chose a parking lot for their rookery. 1. Black skimmer—Juvenile literature. [1. Black skimmer. 2. Birds.]
I. Guravich, Dan, ill. II. Title QL696.C479M38 1990 598'.338—dc20 90-9626 ISBN 0-671-70070-7

SKIMMERS

One day a flock of black-and-white birds circled over a chemical plant in Texas. In the middle of the plant grounds, there was a parking lot covered with crushed oyster shell. The birds landed on the parking lot— right next to the cars. They looked as if they planned to stay there.

The people working at the plant were surprised.

"What kind of birds are those?" a man asked.

"They're black skimmers," another man answered. "I think they must be looking for a place to nest."

He told his fellow workers all he knew about the birds. He explained that a black skimmer has black feathers on its back and head. The feathers on its stomach and throat are white. Skimmers eat fish. When they go fishing, they skim low over the surface of the water. That's why they are called *skimmers.*

The lower half of a skimmer's bill is longer than the upper half. When a skimmer fishes, the lower half of its bill trails through the water. As soon as its bill touches a small fish, the skimmer closes its beak and catches the fish. The bird then raises its head, lifting the fish out of the water. It turns the fish with its tongue so that it can swallow the food headfirst.

Because a skimmer can fish by feel, it can feed at night when other birds cannot. That's how skimmers get plenty to eat.

To catch their food, skimmers must live near the ocean. They rest and sleep on beaches of sand and broken sea shells. For most of the year skimmers use beaches all the way from New York to Mexico. But in the spring they get together in flocks to mate and lay eggs.

At the age of three years, skimmers are old enough to become parents. When it is time for them to start a family, a male will stand near a female. The female flies into the air and he follows. She soars higher and higher, faster and faster. Wherever she goes, the male goes too. He proves that he can fly as well as she can. Only then does she accept him as a mate. They stay together as mates for as long as they both live.

As soon as the female skimmer has eggs growing in her body, she begins looking for a safe place to nest. A birds' nesting place is called a *rookery*. Female skimmers choose the spot where their rookery will be. They prefer an island in the sea or a sand bar surrounded on three sides by water. This helps to keep out unfriendly animals.

Each female chooses a spot for her own nest. She picks a place that is clean and dry. She also makes sure that the nest will be at least six feet away from other nests. When she finds a spot that suits her, she scrapes away the shell or sand and makes a shallow hole. This is called her *scrape*. It must be about eight inches across and two inches deep in the center. She makes it by herself.

As soon as the scrape is ready, she lays her first egg. It is about half the size of a hen's egg—speckled with gray and black spots. It looks so much like the bits of shell around it that a hungry animal might never notice it.

The female skimmer lays one egg a day. She may lay only three eggs if food has been scarce. Or she may lay as many as six eggs if she has had plenty to eat.

The mother and father skimmer take turns sitting on the eggs. This is called *brooding*. The parents must keep the eggs warm during the cool night. They must keep them cool during the hot day. If the bright sun shines steadily on the eggs for just five minutes, the chick growing inside will get so hot that it will die. Several times a day parent skimmers turn the eggs over. They do this to warm or cool them evenly and to help the chicks inside to grow properly.

While one parent broods the eggs, the other flies to the sea to catch fish to eat. After nearly three weeks, the parents hear sounds coming from inside the eggs. The chicks are ready to hatch.

The first egg to be laid is the first to hatch. The chick breaks open the shell from the inside. This is called *pipping*. The chick uses an egg tooth on top of its bill to pip the egg. The tiny hatchling makes the hole wider and wider. Finally, the shell breaks in two, and the chick tumbles out.

Within an hour the chick is dry and standing up. It is covered with fuzzy gray feathers. The feathers have black spots that match the oyster shells all around the scrape. The two halves of the chick's bill are the same length.

After the chick hatches, its egg tooth falls off its bill. The chick doesn't need it anymore. In just half a day, the chick begins to walk around the scrape. It gets acquainted with its parents. It starts to learn what the world is like.

Soon the chick begins to feel hungry. It runs to one of its parents, spreading out its wings. It does a little series of steps with its feet. Then it picks up a bit of oyster shell with its bill and drops it in front of its parent. This tells the parent that the chick wants something to eat.

While one parent guards the chick and the unhatched eggs, the other flies to the sea. There it catches a fish, bringing it back in its bill. First the parent crushes the fish so the chick can swallow it easily. But before the parent gives a chick the fish, the chick spreads its wings and goes through the same series of movements as before. This helps the parent know that the chick is its own. When the chick opens its mouth wide, the parent drops in the fish.

Each day another chick hatches. But not all eggs hatch and not all chicks grow up. A storm may fill the scrape with rainwater. If this happens, a pipped egg can fill with water. Then the chick inside may drown. A raccoon or a fox may take eggs or chicks to eat. Other birds, such as gulls or grackles, often eat skimmer eggs. Sometimes people drive their cars over the beach, destroying rookeries and nests. Or they let their dogs chase the birds and kill the chicks.

Parent skimmers try hard to protect their eggs and chicks. After the eggs have hatched, the mother picks up the empty pieces of shell and carries them away from the scrape. This prevents their attracting enemies.

If a person goes too near a rookery, adult skimmers may attack him. They may try to scratch or peck his head. They want to make the intruder go away. The chicks lie flat against the ground. The coloring of their feathers looks just like the shells and sand that surround them.

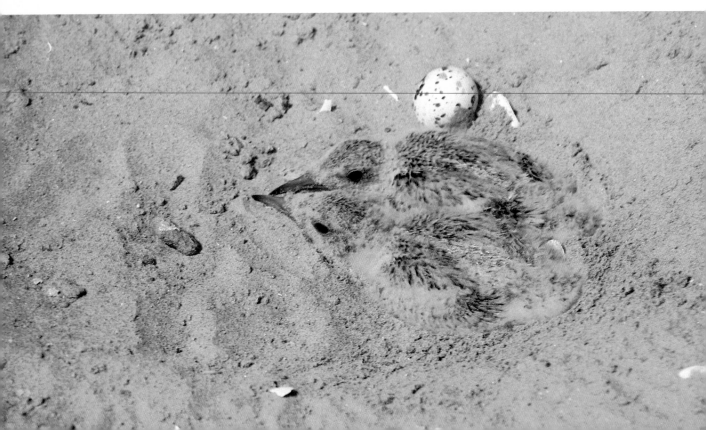

Sometimes a parent bird plays tricks to keep other animals from finding the scrape. It will pretend that it has a broken wing. It crawls away from the scrape crying and dragging its wing on the ground. The animal forgets about the eggs and chicks and chases after the adult bird instead.

Skimmer chicks grow very fast. They learn fast, too. When a strange bird flies overhead, the chicks hide. They stay very still and quiet. Sometimes chicks wander over to other parent skimmers and ask for food. Usually they get a peck that tells them to go back to their own scrape.

At the end of 25 days the chicks have grown to be as big as their parents. Their flying feathers have grown in. They are no longer chicks. They have become fledglings, ready to fly.

The young skimmers watch their parents fly and try to imitate them. They face into the wind and spread their wings. They jump up into the air, flapping their wings. Sure enough, they find that they can fly. They also discover that it is easy to take off, but harder to land. Sometimes they do a belly flop on the sand or bump into other birds. But they practice every day, and their flying skills grow as their muscles get stronger.

Gradually their bills grow longer. The lower bill becomes longer than the upper bill. Now the fledgling must learn to fish and feed itself. The young birds watch while their parents skim over the water, catching fish. When the fledglings try to do it themselves, they discover it is not so easy to fly at just the right distance above the water. It is also difficult to fly with just the lower half of the bill in the water. Sometimes the young skimmers get too close to the water and fall in. Often they catch the wrong things, such as pieces of floating wood. Or they catch fish, then let them get away.

While the young skimmers are learning, their parents continue to feed them. The fledglings practice every day. Before long, they are catching fish, too.

When the young skimmers have finished learning to fly and fish, the flock leaves the rookery. They move up and down the seashore, looking for food. But when spring returns, the flock gets together and goes back to the same rookery.

Sometimes, though, they find that people and their cars have taken over the beaches where they used to nest. So the birds have been forced to squeeze into small strips of sand between a highway and a beach or alongside a causeway leading to a bridge.

After learning more about the habits of skimmers, the astonished employees at the chemical plant began to understand why the flock had landed on their parking lot. Someone or something had probably taken over the birds' usual rookery. In their search for a new spot, they must have settled on the parking lot because it looked like an island, and it was covered with crushed shells. But this "island" was surrounded by a chemical plant instead of water. Even so, the skimmers liked it. For them it was a safe place to lay their eggs. And there was water close at hand.

Some of the workers at the plant wanted to chase the flock away. "We need our parking lot more than we need a bunch of skimmers," they said. But most of them wanted to help the skimmers. They pointed out that there was another parking lot nearby.

The owners of the chemical plant agreed that the skimmers could stay. They put up signs telling people that the parking lot was now a skimmer rookery. One sign warned: Baby skimmers have the right of way.

The skimmers seemed to appreciate their welcome. Every year they returned to their unusual Texas rookery. In time, the flock grew to number 2,000 birds. Each year they hatched and raised about 800 chicks there.

The skimmer rookery in the chemical plant grounds became famous. Many people came to see it. And each year the company held a party next to the rookery. Parents brought their children to drink lemonade and eat cookies and see the baby skimmers. People were pleased that the company allowed the birds to have a rookery right on the plant grounds. It proved that they could produce birds as well as chemicals. They were helping to make sure that skimmers continued to live and thrive.